THE
BOOK OF
WISECRACKS

THE BOOK OF WISECRACKS

Windows of wisdom for living well

GERALD MANN

Riverbend Press

Austin, Texas 78746

Copyright © 1998 by Gerald Mann

Published by: Riverbend Press, Austin, Texas

Library of Congress
Catalog Card Number (*Applied For*)
ISBN 0-9647272-1-8

10 9 8 7 6 5 4 3 2 1

Printed in the United States of America

For two of the Magi:
George Payne, my unlettered mentor,
and Anna Maria, *angel de la
guarda de mi familia.*

CONTENTS

From the Author

This gathering of rhymes and ruminations is for people who want to live well in *this* world.

They are based more on spirituality than religion. Religion concerns itself mostly with getting to heaven and escaping damnation.

I certainly endorse these worthy concerns, but this work is about translating reverence for God, as I understand Him, into everyday real life. *Spirituality,* as I'm using the term, means I am essentially a spiritual being living in a material world, and that life makes sense only when I live from the *inside out,* i.e., when I allow the spiritual source of my being to interpret and govern how I live.

For these reasons, I chose the Old Testament book of Proverbs as the resource for this collection. It is a "this world" book. It concerns itself with how to live wholesomely (as a whole person) *now.*

It bases all of its advice on this premise: Reverence for God is the beginning of wisdom. Wisdom is not a matter of possessing information. It's the art of living skillfully in all conditions because of being anchored to a spiritual base. In short, *wisdom* and *spirituality* are synonyms.

You will discover immediately that my rendering of Solomon's Proverbs differs from those in your Bible. There are two reasons. First, the various translations of Proverbs from Hebrew to English are quite different themselves. I used six translations in preparing this collection, and no one of them reads exactly like any other.

Second, I am more concerned with what the Bible *means* than with what it *says*. Every human language has different nuances that cannot be translated word for word and carry the same meaning. Also, individual languages change their meanings over time. For example, the King James English contains phraseology that, in order to make sense to us, needs translating into modern English.

At any rate, my goal was not to render an exact conversion from Hebrew into English, or from King James English into modern English, but to convert ancient meanings into modern meanings. As resources, I used *The Hebrew Bible*, *The King James Version*, *The Revised Berkeley Version in Modern English*, *The Good News Bible*, *The Revised Standard Version* and *The Message*, by Eugene Peterson.

Two more things. I chose to convert the meaning of the proverbs into rhymes, which I call "Wisecracks," so that I could remember them more easily—not to exhibit any poetic talent. The rhymes are "light verse," with a heavy emphasis on the word *light!*

Finally, you will notice that there is no effort to

present the Wisecracks in a systematic fashion—and that I end them at Proverbs 22. This choice was based on the nature of the book of Proverbs itself. The major section of the book (1:1–22:16) contains the proverbs of Solomon, son of David. The remaining sections, for the most part, simply repeat Solomon's teaching. Also Solomon's proverbs themselves are not systematically arranged. He jumps from one subject to another, and I have followed suit.

Gerald Mann

Reverence for God is the beginning of Wisdom ...

~Proverbs 1:7

Proverbs 1:1

The proverbs of Solomon, son of David ...

1
You *Can* Begin Again!

Wisecrack
David saw Bathsheba bathing
and received a proper scathing
for the wrongs that glance inspired.
But from the ashes of his deed,
there flowered yet another seed:
the wisest son that e'er was sired.

Moralizers are faithful to remind us that King David's life was all downhill following Bathshebagate. They list a litany of his woes:

- The baby of his illicit union died.
- He confessed publicly, daring to call his actions "sins," but he never recovered his moral stature with the people.
- His sons fought over succession. One was beheaded for trying to dethrone him.
- God deprived him of his grandest dream—building the Temple. Too much blood on his hands.

The opening words of the book of Proverbs should

forever silence such sanctimony.

Solomon, the fountain of God's wisdom, sprang from the womb and loins of two people who had adulterated their person and privilege. For all of David's heroic feats—giant-killing, kingdom-consolidating, hymn-writing—his single greatest achievement was the son of his old age. Solomon is a monument of contradiction to all naysaying moralists of the ages.

Where else did Solomon get his insight, far-sight and foresight, but at the knees of two broken souls who had been mended by the fires of forgiveness and the grace of a second chance?

Oh, but you *can* begin again after your Bathshebagates!

Where else
did Solomon get
his insight, far-sight
and foresight, but
at the knees of
two broken souls
who had been
mended by
the fires of
forgiveness and
the grace of a
second chance?

~Gerald Mann

Proverbs 1:8-9

Children, listen to what your father
and mother tell you.
What they learned will be like
flowers in your hair
and rings on your fingers.
Wear their experience like clothes
to beautify your character.

2
Scarred Warriors Make Good Teachers

Wisecrack

When it was my turn, they tried to tell me,
but I wouldn't take counsel and I couldn't see.
With the bit in my teeth, it was full-speed ahead,
and I became wise just in time to be dead.
Now it's your turn to take counsel
and your time to see,
but why should you listen to someone like me?
Because—and I say without pause—
my scars are well-earned and cannot be hid,
so, do what I learned. *Don't do what I* did.

We hide the sins of our youth from our children for fear they'll repeat them. Why do we imagine they won't discover our feet of clay just as we discovered those of our parents?

Why are we so convinced that *information* and *causation* are synonymous? ("If they *know* how, they'll *do* it.") Truth is, they're going to do it, with or without knowhow!

When the hormones start howling, information is one of their and your best allies. Confession, too. It humanizes you. Kids relate best to flesh-and-blood parents.

But, you say, who are we to tell them not to inhale and to keep their legs crossed, when we did the opposite? The best-qualified advisors they'll ever have, that's who!

If every generation aped its parents, we'd still be apes. Our evolution depends on learning from the mistakes of our forefathers. Every time we refuse to listen to our history, it repeats itself.

Our hope is that our children will do what we learned, not what we did.

My

scars are
well-earned and
cannot be hid,
so do what
I learned.
Don't do
what I did.

~Gerald Mann

Proverbs 1:10-18

When peers entice you to do wrong,
don't be naïve.
Look for the telltale signs of losers.
They'll say "Come on! Let's rob and
kill the honest people.
We'll get rich quick and share
the loot like one family."
Lose these losers!
They are driven by the obsession
to have everything now.
They can't wait. They can't even pause.
They're in a mad rush toward ruin.
Even a bird will avoid a trap
he sees being set for him.
But losers don't even notice the deathtraps
they're setting for themselves.
They are lying in wait
to consume their own blood.

3

The Three Laws of Losers

Wisecrack

You can't peg a winner 'til the race is done
nor love the winning hearts of those
who gave their best but never won.
But pegging losers is an easy one.
They embrace the laws of losing
'ere the race is run.

What are the three laws of losers?

1. *Losers love company.* If misery loves company, so does malice. The best way to salve a guilty conscience is to recruit a partner in crime. Shared guilt stings less. "Come on! Let's rob and kill.... We'll ... share the loot like one family" (Proverbs 1:11-13).

2. *Losers worship the shortcut.* They are driven by immediacy. For example, they want riches. Instead of taking the time to acquire them by conventional means, they rob. Or, they want an attractive woman. Instead of taking the time to pursue and wed, they rape. "Lose these losers! They are driven by the obsession to have everything now" (Proverbs 1:15-16).

3. *Losers cannibalize themselves.* They are like the mythical starving man who consumed parts of his body to stay alive: first a finger, then a hand. Self-consumption is a loser's law. "They are lying in wait to consume their own blood" (Proverbs 1:18).

If misery loves company, so does malice. The best way to salve a guilty conscience is to recruit a partner in crime.

~Gerald Mann

Proverbs 1:20-33

Lady Wisdom calls out to everyone
everywhere in everyday life.
"How long will you worship knowledge
and hate wisdom?" she cries.
"How long will you ignore
the realm of the sacred?
I wanted to make you as wise as you are smart,
but you smirked at the idea of reverence.
All right, then. We'll see who laughs last.
A day will come when it will
take wisdom to survive.
Knowledge without reverence won't work.
You'll need to think on your feet
when calamity strikes,
but you will be clueless.
Smugness will kill the shrewd.
Complacency will murder the clever.
But those who have heeded my call
will stand safely against the storm."

4
Get Smart or Get Wise?

Wisecrack
Those whom we dub the quick-witted
were by no means naturally fitted
to become the cultural elite.
It's only by learning to think on their seat
they develop the skill to think on their feet.

Contrary to popular opinion, the difference between being smart and being wise has nothing to do with age. *Wisdom* is not merely "seasoned intelligence." Age makes smart people more clever, more shrewd, but it doesn't make them wise. Wisdom comes from reverence. It begins with a sense of awe and wonder toward transcendence.

The beginning of wisdom is the fear of the Lord. *Fear* means "a sacred respect, or reverence, for the majesty of all that is." The *Lord* means "a power higher than I—one I can only revere and barely comprehend." Supreme mystery.

Socrates exhibited this reverence. He said that he *absolutely knew* only one thing: that he was ignorant.

17

Yet we humans seem bent on worshiping knowledge and hating wisdom. We hurry to confine reality to what we can perceive with our limited senses and prove with our puny methods.

We exclude the realm of the sacred from our public discourse. Our modern education has no place for reverence. Marriage, sex and child-rearing have become casualized. *Philosophy* ("the love of wisdom") has abandoned its search for ultimate reality and confined itself to analyzing language.

Just as the proverb says, we smirk at reverence, and the result is that we are unprepared to face adversity. We can't think on our feet, roll with the punches, adapt and adjust—because we haven't acquired wisdom.

To acquire wisdom, you must stop ... and sit ... and wonder.

To acquire wisdom, you must stop ... and sit ... and wonder.

~Gerald Mann

Proverbs 2:2-9

Keep your ear to the ground for wisdom.
Let your heart race for understanding.
Cry out for insight. Search for it as
you would for a buried treasure.
Let nothing get in your way.
If you do this, something
amazing will happen.
God's thinking will find you!
You'll wake up one day and
know His heart and will and mind!
You will be shielded and
protected by common sense,
and you will be able to recognize
the right, the just and the fair.

5

Craving What We Already Have

Wisecrack

Those who rant and pant and lurch
to find a God who's there for sure
should not expect to end their search
with a beatific vision pure.
Nor should their failure cause despair.
Their longing proves that God is there.

If you're hankering for God, He's already found you, for it is God who creates the hankering. If He weren't already with you, He'd never cross your mind.

But searching for God can also make you sick, if what you really want is an irrefutable proof of God that will put to rest all of your doubts, once and for all. God will not submit Himself to the canons of your reason. He won't become your household pet. He will not dance for your doubts.

What *can* you expect? You can expect to know God's mind in matters of the right and the just and the fair. You can expect to be shielded from foolishness by God-given common sense.

It's good to pant and rant and lurch for a pure vision of God ... as long as you don't expect your search to end in your possessing Him.

It is He who does the possessing.

If you're
hankering
for God, He's
already found
you, for it is
God who creates
the hankering.

~Gerald Mann

Proverbs 2:10-15

When wisdom becomes your mistress,
your knowledge will give you the
greatest of all pleasures—serenity.
Serenity keeps you from following
dead-end streets.
It enables you to resist fools who have
confused cheap thrills with deep joy.
It will keep you from running off
with seducers.

6
But the Greatest
of These ...

Wisecrack
We treasure pleasure in any measure,
though its fires abate with perfidy.
But there is a bliss that's blind to time,
a soul-deep flame—serenity.

Do you know the difference between *fun* and *joy*? If you don't, I can't explain it to you. If you do, I don't have to.

But I can illustrate it. Fun is the rushing warmth of wine metabolizing. Fun is the faint tightening of the line before the explosion of a fish on the hook. There are countless triggers of the orgiastic sensations we call "fun."

Joy is different.

It is hearing my child say my name for the first time. It's watching four generations of my family open their gifts at Christmas time. It's watching Americans of all color, creed and cause view fireworks on July 4. Not the fireworks ... the *people*. The fireworks bring fun. People, united in a common moment that erases all differences, bring joy.

All sane humans experience both fun and joy. They are native to our existence. But there is another state that isn't native. It must be acquired.

Serenity.

Serenity is a by-product. You can't create it, discover it, conjure it up. It happens when you allow wisdom to enter your heart, i.e., when wisdom "becomes your mistress."

Serenity is a by-product of letting go—of leaving ownership of the self to a higher power.

The dominant result of serenity is safety. It's what poets and seers often call "inner harmony."

Solomon was more practical in his description of serenity:

1. *It keeps you from wasting steps following dead-end streets.* Serene people are not afraid they'll "miss something."

2. *It enables you to resist fools who don't know the difference between cheap thrills and deep joy.*

3. *It enables you to spot seducers.* A seducer wants you to do what's good for him and bad for you. But serenity sees what's good for everybody.

Fun, joy and serenity—we can experience all three. But the greatest of these ...

*Serenity is a
by-product
of letting go~of
leaving ownership
of the self to
a higher power.*

~Gerald Mann

Proverbs 3:1-12

Remember the four *never*s of living well:
• *Never* abandon faithfulness and loyalty.
They are the two *musts* of happy relationships.
• *Never* think you know it all.
Do what you know to be right,
and if in doubt, don't do it.
• *Never* give your best last and your
leftovers first. Do just the opposite.
This is the only way to enjoy wealth.
• *Never* confuse correction with rejection.
God corrects us because He loves us …
as a proud father corrects
the child of his delight.

7
The *Never*s
that Never Fail

Wisecrack

No matter the steepness of the climb,
nor the fierceness of the gale,
throughout the tests of woe and time,
choose the "nevers" that never fail.

The quest for permanence is the yearning of the human soul. We are mortal creatures, and we know it. To know our impermanence is also to perceive the possibility of permanence.

This is our human dilemma: As citizens of two worlds—time and eternity, matter and spirit, heaven and earth—how can we find moments of permanent meaning in the midst of our transience? Are there *never*s that never fail?

Yes! There are four qualities *never* to abandon:

1. *A loyal heart.* "At-one-ness" with another person (love) heals our transient nature. We can stop time with friends, lovers, family and community—but only if we learn and practice loyalty.

Loyalty consists of two elements—forgiveness and reliability. All relationships are doomed without the element of forgiveness because all lovers are imperfect. Reliability—fidelity—is the only anchor we have when the climb is steep and the gale is fierce. You matter, if only one other person in the world is *there* for you.

2. *A hungry mind.* To realize you're not "in the know," and therefore to be constantly "on the know," has a permanence of its own. He who knows it all is dead already. To be hungry to know is to be alive.

3. *A generous hand.* The dumbest of all mistakes is our attempt to gain permanence through accumulating *things.* We can gain power, prestige, pride and pleasure by cranking up the zeros. But meaning and money can be connected only through *giving.*

We gain the permanence we seek when we pass on our *things* to others. You can't take it with you, but you can send *you* with it!

However, that advice doesn't work with leftovers. Giving away leftovers is like giving away the sleeves of a vest. Having wealth is always *fun* (despite warnings to the contrary), but having wealth is a *joy* only when we have a drain plug for greed.

4. *A teachable spirit.* Bad things happen to good people because bad things happen to *all* people. The bad times remind us, like nothing else, of our mortality. Cancer is an equal-opportunity destroyer. Tornadoes don't check IDs.

Yet, suffering can be our greatest opportunity to experience permanence *if—If* we embrace suffering as correction instead of rejection. *If* we ask "What am I to learn through this?" instead of "Why me?"

Why me? is a strange question anyway. Everything else that lives is terminal. Why *not* me?

The spirit that dares to learn by suffering outlives the suffering.

*Y*ou can't take it with you, but you can send you with it!

~Gerald Mann

Proverbs 3:27-32

Here's how to be a friend to your neighbor:
Don't wait for him to ask you for help
if he obviously needs it.
Don't make him wait if he asks
for help that you can give.
Don't make plans that help you but hurt him.
What happens to him happens to you.
Don't wear a chip on your shoulder.
Neighbors can't keep from disturbing each other.
It goes with the neighborhood.
Don't copy the neighborhood jerk.
Every neighborhood has one. Two is too many.

8
Being a Friend *and* a Neighbor

Wisecrack

Of all the wealth that attends our labor
and all we've won with gun and saber,
the grandest prize to grace our favor
is that rare friend who is also neighbor.

Truism: "Good fences make good neighbors."
Commandment: "Love thy neighbor as thyself."

At first glance, these two seem to offer conflicting advice. The first reminds us to keep a well-marked boundary between us and the guys next door. They are not us, not family.

Yet they are not strangers either. They are next to us, which is what the word *neighbor* means. Therefore, our task is to find a way to befriend neighbors without absorbing them.

When the commandment tells us to love our

neighbors as ourselves, it acknowledges something we often forget—*we have two selves!* "As *you* love *yourself,*" it says—as *you* (your higher self) love *yourself* (your lower self).

Do you keep a boundary between these two selves? I hope so. Otherwise, you are not human. You have no *self* control.

You can see where I'm going with this. The only way to love yourself—*wholesomely*—is to keep a good fence between your higher and lower selves. Your lower self is not an alien. It is your neighbor within. It lives next to you. You can't ignore it and live well. But you can't be absorbed by it, either. So, there's no conflict between these two counsels.

Now the big question: *How do we befriend our neighbor without treading on his sacred ground?*

Solomon gives us four gems of practical advice:

1. *When your neighbor needs help, timing is everything.* Don't wait for him to ask for what he obviously needs. *Be there first!* Let your help beat his request.

2. *Don't put him off when he does ask.* He's embarrassed to ask, for he knows you have what he doesn't. So, *be there quickly!* Treat his request as an emergency. When you're making big changes, sharing information is everything. Your property is your domain, but it's not an island. It is adjoined by your neighbor's domain. Let him be the second to know your plans.

3. *See your neighbor's nuisances as his nuances,*

i.e., as his distinctive nature. Two people can't live next to each other without bothering each other.

Example: My neighbor played rock 'n' roll on Saturdays. I played country music. I became a fan of his music, and he became a fan of mine.

4. *If you live next door to the neighborhood jerk, you have only two viable choices: move, or turn him into a friend.* There is a third response—becoming a jerk, too—but it's not a viable choice. It's a recipe for guaranteed misery. Ever hear of the Hatfields and McCoys? or (if you're more cultured) the Montagues and the Capulets?

*O*ur task
is to find a
way to befriend
neighbors without
absorbing them.

~Gerald Mann

Proverbs 4:1-9

Children, soak up the wisdom of your elders.
When I was very young, my parents began
to recite to me our family story ...
what we learned and who we became
through our ups and downs.
They repeated them over and over. They told
me: Never forget your story, and
never forget the lessons we learned.
Then they told me to pursue new wisdom
with all my might, so that I could
add to what I received and pass it on.
They believed that wisdom was the most
valuable thing they could leave me ...
the only thing that would truly
increase my life and give me glory.

9

It All Happens at Home

Wisecrack

"I have no bread," the father said,
"See my children frail and gaunt?
These I cherish shall not perish
for lack of a champ to sate their want!"
From then to now, he's served this vow
and showers them with largesse.
But he hears within the swelling din
of a voice that fuels a constant stress:
"You've made them puppets on golden strings;
they dance the tune called 'Love Is Things'—
what we have and take and give.
You've taught them how to make a living,
but you haven't taught them how to live."

As goes the family, so goes the culture. If one thing is clear on the eve of the 21st century, it is this maxim.

To survive, civilizations require four functioning institutions: government, education, religion (a spiritual mythology) and family. Oddly enough, the family can survive—even flourish—without the other three. Families function without the imposition of outside authority (government); without public schools (today, home-schooled children scholastically outperform publicly schooled children); and without official religious indoctrination. However, the other three cannot survive without a strong, family-centered culture!

The USSR learned this lesson the hard way. The communists dismantled the traditional nuclear family. Then they rushed to reassemble it, but it was too late. America ignores their failure and dismantles the family for the sake of convenience ... or in the name of liberation.

Voices of alarm finally are being sounded as we drown in a sea of single-parent, unfathered and alternative-model families.

Home is where it happens—

- where we learn how to say "I"—where we learn who we are and what we stand for;
- where we learn to say "we"—where we learn love as commitment and fidelity;
- where we learn to say "thou"—where we learn we're created for more than *stuff*;

and home is, according to Proverbs,

- where we receive love's most valuable inheritance—wisdom.

Home is where all these things happen. It's the only place where they *can* happen.

Home
is where we
receive love's
most valuable
inheritance~
wisdom.

~Gerald Mann

Proverbs 4:20-27

Keep close tabs on the desires of your heart.
Your outward life depends on it.
Straight-talking and straight-walking
come from straight-thinking.
If you lie, gossip, run off at the mouth
and charge ahead with no ethics,
changing your habits won't help.
You're trying to live from the outside in.
Real change begins in the heart—
from the inside out.

10
What Makes a Person "Good"?

Wisecrack

We awaken and ask the coming day's task;
we steel ourselves to fight hidden elves.
We lament interruptions and curse life's distractions,
but have we yet dared to be more than reactions?
We dream of a time when life is sublime;
we yearn without cease for an inner peace.
We crave to be out of this killing drought,
but have we yet dared living from the inside out?

Laws are designed to create order, not goodness. They never made one person better. They merely tell us *who* is "bad" and *when*.

For that reason, the moral strength of a society is inversely proportionate to the number of its laws. The more laws, the weaker the moral character of the society. The more legality, the less morality.

An immoral society reduces "right vs. wrong" to

"legal vs. illegal." One result is the frequently heard statement, "I did nothing wrong ... and I promise I'll never do it again." Another is the metamorphosis of the Supreme Court from judicial interpretation to a NeoCollege of Cardinals.

Morality must always be defined by a higher power. The key question concerning right and wrong is *Who says?* In other words, *Which higher power* is to say what is right and what is wrong?

The person or society that no longer has a God to address must find another authority, i.e., nine robed legal eagles in D.C.

Legality means living from the outside in, as all of the above discussion tells us. We attempt to use outside laws to create moral behavior.

Morality is living from the inside out. "Keep close tabs on the desires of your heart."

"As a man thinketh in his heart, so *is* he."

Legality means living from the outside in … Morality is living from the inside out.

~Gerald Mann

Proverbs 5:3-20

There's nothing like a torrid affair
with a forbidden lover! Lips like honey
… smooth as olive oil … the rush!
At first, anyway. But when reality sets in,
you're left with a flat taste and gnawing guilt.
You've gone down a road to
a dead place in your soul. You've lost
a part of yourself you can't retrieve.
So hear this, even if you don't heed it.
Stay out of adultery's neighborhood!
Don't expose yourself to temptation!
Once you cross the line, there's no turning back.
And in the end, you will be estranged … from
others and from the self you once knew.
Remember the old saying: "Drink from your
own barrel. Draw from your own well.
Let your children be the wellspring of your love,
not the offspring of your lust."
So, love the one you married. You have
everything at home to build a great sex life.
Why look for someone to *use* when
you have someone to *enjoy*?

11
Straight Facts—
Sexual Fantasies

Wisecrack

Have you paused to ponder the ironic wonder
of the advance of the hominid?
As a beast, breeding strangers, he learned of the
dangers of life without mate and kid.
Through trial and error, he emerged from the terror
to a state of civility.
His surest anchor against chaos and rancor
was a hearth and a home and a family.
But when he became the master of earth,
the crown of intellectual evolution,
he returned to the precincts
of his primitive instincts,
and called it a "sexual revolution."

Solomon certainly knew what he was talking about when
it came to adultery. Why shouldn't he? His parents were
the most celebrated adulterers in history. The words in
these proverbs are, no doubt, straight from David's

mouth.

But are they relevant today? Is there really any use in talking about an exclusive sexual union, with one person, "till death (or divorce) do us part"?

I mean, haven't the advent of the pill, the liberation of women from the status of property and the prolongation of adolescence, along with the dual focus on love without commitment and sex as recreation, made the biblical prescriptions about adultery obsolete?

To tell the truth, I wish it were so. If God and nature and societal health would cancel the seventh commandment, we could happily call fantasy reality and be done with it. It won't work.

God and religion aside, marriage and fidelity are here to stay—else *we* are not! Sexual monogamy is not an ecclesiastical invention. It is an evolutionary necessity. A society is in trouble when it can no longer tell the difference between fantasy and reality regarding sexual behavior. This being so, Solomon's advice is as solid today as ever.

Solomon gives us three straight facts about sexual fantasies:

1. *Variety is the* ice *of life.* Chasing strange always ends in estrangement. Most people don't believe this until after they've tested it. No matter. It's still true. Because sex with strangers is *using,* not sharing. Long-lasting sexual gratification occurs between lovers who are also friends and companions.

2. *Repression creates* progression, *not depression.*

There is no correlation between sexual restraint and neurosis. There is definitely a correlation between *loneliness* and neurosis. But sexual release doesn't cure loneliness. Using sex to bond with another person cures loneliness. Using another person sexually increases loneliness.

3. *Sex is for* soul *mates, not playmates*. To reduce sex to "play," as in a game of tennis or scrabble (except with more pleasure, of course), is to cheapen the concept of play. If you need this one explained, you'll never grasp it.

*S*ex
is for
soul mates,
not playmates.

~Gerald Mann

Proverbs 6:1-5

Have you made a rash
commitment you can't keep?
Promised something you can't deliver?
The only way out is to act quickly.
Don't prolong the misery. Swallow
your pride, 'fess up, cut your losses.
Don't stop to think about it. Flee like
a deer from the hunter.

12
For Promise-Breakers

Wisecrack
Is anything worse
than a promise unkept,
whether done with aforethought
or by talents inept?
Yea, one thing is worse,
more sinister and mean:
to know you can't keep it
and refuse to come clean.

Promises are not guarantees. They are based upon assumptions which have yet to materialize. Therefore, they always involve leaps of faith in ourselves and in circumstances. This is why many get broken. Often, circumstances beyond our control intervene.

But broken promises hurt. They score the souls of people and of society. Cynicism, apathy, selfishness, infidelity and crime—all are symptoms of sick souls who no longer believe promises. The low estate of American political life is a case in point. Politicians make bogus promises to people who will not elect them if they don't make the promises. And some people are still amazed when elected officials turn out to be adulterers!

Nevertheless, most promises can be kept and are. Otherwise, society would be paralyzed. We couldn't buy groceries, fuel or medicine if we didn't trust the promises on the labels. We couldn't work productively if our employer's promise to pay wasn't valid. And even though we lament the breakdown of the family, the truth is that most of us experience enough promises kept to survive.

But there is one kind of broken promise that's hardest to overcome: one broken long before it comes to light. Our ability to process betrayal is directly proportionate to the length of time that elapses before we know we've been had. If we know quickly, we can get through it and get on with it. But being the last to know we've been betrayed is a killer.

It's inevitable we all will become promise-breakers. But the extent of the damage is up to us. It depends on our courage and our quickness to confess.

*C*ynicism,
apathy,
selfishness,
infidelity and crime~
all are symptoms
of sick souls
who no longer
believe promises....
Nevertheless, most
promises can
be kept and are.

~Gerald Mann

Proverbs 6:16-19

There are seven things God hates:
eyes that are arrogant,
a tongue that lies,
hands that kill the innocent,
a heart that plots evil,
feet that hurry to do evil,
a mouth that distorts reality,
a spirit that divides people.

13
Seven Habits of God-Feeling People

Wisecrack

For way too long, we've had God all wrong.
We've seen Him as ourselves enlarged.
Especially when it comes to hate,
we've given Him our human trait,
except with zeal divinely charged.
In truth, His wrath is not, like ours,
a wanton, driven urge to maim.
It is that part of God's dear heart
that aches to call us from our shame.
God's wrath is real, but it's what we feel
when all His pleas have been rejected
and He has to leave us to ourselves—
alone, confused and unprotected.

God's hate is mentioned in the Bible enough to give violent people the excuse they need to hurt others in His name, but—except for the very primitive passages—His "hate" is nothing like ours.

53

First of all, it is passive. It's what we feel when we've developed habits that exclude Him from the inner recesses of our lives. And what we feel is— *emptiness!* Pain, tragedy, illness and ill fortune are not God's hatred in action. His "hatred" is His *absence,* caused by our stubbornness! As the Scripture reiterates: "He keeps quiet and lets us draw our own confusions."

Proverbs 6:16-19 lists seven things God hates. These are the seven habits or traits that bar Him from our hearts ... that prevent us from feeling His presence.

When we *reverse* these seven, state them positively, we discover seven habits that allow us to feel God on a daily basis.

So, here are the seven habits of God-feeling people:

1. *God-feeling people look wistfully.* The ancients believed that the *eyes* revealed one's hunger for God. Arrogant eyes say, "no need for God." But wistful eyes reveal a hunger to know more and more. They reveal those who are "poor in spirit," as opposed to "puffed up" in spirit.

2. *God-feeling people talk transparently.* The *tongue* is the doorkeeper of one's inward integrity. A "tongue that lies" lets out deception and duplicity. It hides the inner self's intentions and stops God at the door. But a tongue that "talks transparently" lets out the true inner self. People who talk transparently are the ones Jesus called the "pure in heart."

3. *God-feeling people work "empowering-fully."* *Hands* were seen as the extensions or tools of a person's power to create and pass on his work … or to destroy. Thus, "hands that kill the innocent" means more than killing noncombatants. It means using one's life force to diminish the world. The opposite would be to "work empowering-fully." God can be present only in the life that is ambitious to *em*power others, not *over*power them.

4. *God-feeling people think glad-heartedly.* The *heart* was seen as the command post of all personhood. ("As a man thinketh in his heart, so *is* he.") The heart was the "plotting room" of one's life. We moderns would substitute the mind. Naturally, "the heart that plots evil" has all doors to God sealed off. Its opposite would be the heart that plots goodness, or joy, for everyone.

Jesus battled with religious folk who had no place for gladness in their hearts. Their religion plotted only burdens and negatives. God-feeling people are glad-hearted people.

5. *God-feeling people hurry reverently.* *Feet* were one's tools of urgency. They revealed what people were anxious for, what they hurried to do. Thus, God is said to hate feet that *hurry* to do evil.

Why? Because they have excluded reverence for God and for others from the category of urgency. God has been shut out of what's most important.

But feet that "hurry reverently" lead people to priorities like prayer, meditation and quality time with family and friends.

If you have no time for God, time *is* your God.

6. God-feeling people "transmit" bravely. The *mouth* was seen as the shaper of reality. It was the molder of honesty and dishonesty. It transmitted reality, just as a witness tells a jury the way it really was. When God is said to hate "the mouth that lies under oath," distortion of truth is the topic. The opposite, then, is the mouth that dares to transmit what really happened, i.e., the unvarnished truth: "Nothing but the facts, Ma'am."

God-feeling people are the ones who bravely stick to the facts and faithfully pass them on to posterity.

7. God-feeling people love inclusively. The *spirit,* in ancient thought, governed personal relationships with God and with others. One's spirit defined friend and enemy. "God loathes a spirit that divides people," says Proverbs. He can't connect with rabble-rousers, those who think in "us vs. them" categories. Exclusionists.

God-feeling people love inclusively. "Blessed are the peacemakers. They shall be called the children of God."

But how does all this square with Jesus' words in Matthew 10, where he says he has come to divide fathers and sons, to bring a "sword" between people, and so on?

It squares very easily. In that text, he was about to send his disciples on their first mission. He was warning them not to expect exclusionists to welcome them!

Exclusionists hate inclusionists. When you dare to make God everyone's father, you had better be prepared to catch heat from those who think He belongs only to them.

If
you have
no time
for God,
time is your
God.

~Gerald Mann

Proverbs 6:6-8

Learn from the lowly ant. It will teach you two
important lessons about meaningful work.
First: It does what needs to be done
without considering who's in charge.
Second: It stockpiles provisions in summer
so that its colony can survive in winter.

14

On Finding Decent Help

Wisecrack

How long must we suffer that incessant yelp:
"These days you just can't find decent help"?
They wail as though their plight were new,
but since Adam left Eden it's always been true.
Good workers are scarce, but by no means extinct,
and they all share two traits that make them distinct:
• Their focus is on what needs to be done,
not who will turn out to be number one.
• Their purpose is cast with an eye on posterity,
not on the fruits of personal prosperity.

Enjoyment of work has little to do with how much money, power or acclaim it brings us. Right?

We really don't believe this, of course. But it's true, nonetheless! People who find meaning in their labor have two things going for them.

1. When facing a task, they refuse to ask such questions as: "What will happen to me? Who will get the blame if the project fails? the credit, if it succeeds?

Am I being exploited? Is this work ultimately fulfilling?"

Behind all these questions is the false assumption that my work should *make* me somebody, that I *am* what I *do,* that all work should enhance my personhood. Not so. Work will never make me into somebody if I don't already *feel* that I am somebody.

Instead, people who enjoy their work focus on one simple question—"What needs to be done here?" Their meaning comes from creating and completing, without regard for self.

2. *People who enjoy work are like the ant in Proverbs.* They see work *primarily* as a contribution to the preservation of the colony in the future, rather than to their own preservation.

Two questions to ask yourself:

• "Am I working to *do something* or to *be somebody*?"
• "Am I working for *posterity* or for *prosperity?*"

Winter is on its way. Even an ant knows this. And winter cares nothing for rank and summer prosperity.

Work will never make me into somebody if I don't already feel that I am somebody.

~Gerald Mann

Proverbs 7:6-27

As I stood watching young men
on the streets one night,
I spied one who was especially naïve.
When he came to one corner, he was
approached by a well-known beauty.
She was dressed provocatively
and making plans. She caressed him and
cooed her lines. He looked startled,
but intrigued. Then he looked like an ox
being led to the slaughter.
He followed after her like a deer in rut,
who pays no attention to the hunter.
Listen up, guys! This is for you.
You're sexually wired in such a way
that you can't turn back once you
give in to an aggressive woman like that.
She has more notches on her gun
than you can count. She's brought down
stronger men than you. Enter her bedroom,
and you're already halfway to hell.

15
No Contest

Wisecrack

In olden times we dared believe:
• that chastity was up to Eve;
• that Adam was a lowly beast
(if offered fare, he could but feast);
• that society could not withstand
a woman acting like a man.
Then we deemed this lowly scheme,
a chauvinistic machination
and called for Eve's just liberation.
Now in the shadow of that declaration,
we shriek with holy indignation
at any voice that dares proclaim that
human nature is still the same—
that Eve's dispensing of her pleasure,
is still a nation's moral measure.

We do indeed shriek at the hint that sexual promiscuity
in a society is in any way connected to women's moral
standards. For eons, a woman was chattel; she kept her

virginity only as an economic advantage to the man who owned her.

Men have always been promiscuous because they have had the freedom to be so. Now that women have been freed to self-determination, how dare *anyone* suggest they be the barometers of sexual morality?!

All too true! Nowhere does the Bible suggest a double standard, i.e., "boys will be boys" and girls must guard the gates of chastity.

However, the Bible does more than suggest that, in a so-called "equal sexual chase," a woman has the upper hand. When women are as free as men to be sexually aggressive, it's hardly a contest—the prey has become the predator.

All these ideas say two things to us moderns:

1. *Men need to recognize that they are the "weaker sex" when it comes to temptations.* Whether this is the result of centuries of cultural conditioning or something hormonal, it seems undeniable.

2. *While women are celebrating their new-found and well-deserved rights, they should respect the rights of other women.* The Tenth Commandment needs amending to add: "Thou shalt not covet another woman's husband, or her livestock, or her house or anything else that is hers."

It *is* a double standard if men alone are excused from sexual fidelity. But it's *also* a double standard to excuse female infidelity as some kind of sick recompense for centuries of discrimination.

While women are celebrating their new-found and well-deserved rights, they should respect the rights of other women. The 10th Commandment needs amending to add: "Thou shalt not covet another woman's husband …"

~Gerald Mann

Proverbs 10:1

A wise son makes his father proud;
a foolish one makes his mother grieve.

16
The Real Difference
Between Moms & Dads

Wisecrack
How different the reactions
to my stupid actions
on the part of my Mom and my Dad!
She goes and cries;
he drops his eyes.
Have I died, or have I just been bad?

A father envisions his children as extensions of his *prowess.* He hopes they'll achieve what he has or more; that they'll reach heights he dreamed of but never scaled. He hopes to excel vicariously through them.

They are extensions of his *doing.* That's why their failures wound his pride, and their successes puff him up.

A dad takes a child's failure as a shaming event.

For mothers, children are extensions of their *being.* Formed in her body, their lives are her *life.* When they act foolishly, they are robbing her of *life*.

Thus the ancient proverb is not as silly as it first appears.

A wise son makes his father proud—he takes the place of his old man in *doing*.

A foolish son makes his mother grieve—she sees his folly as a death in her *being*.

A father
envisions his
children as extensions
of his doing.
For mothers,
children are extensions
of their being.

~Gerald Mann

Proverbs 10:3
God won't allow the honest to stay hungry
or the dishonest to ever be full.

17
When Plenty Is
Never Enough

Wisecrack

Reaching for more is an unavoidable sore
that plagues the human condition.
And though resolute, our honest pursuit
often turns into greedy ambition.
How to tell when our souls we would sell
for the sake of more and more stuff?
When we worship our wants instead of our needs,
and plenty is never enough.

We all lament human greed, yet rarely do we see ourselves as part of the problem. We point to those who have a lot, want more and will stop at nothing to get it. The news keeps the blatantly greedy in the spotlight. Children murder parents, and vice versa, for money.

We also point to those who don't have a lot, claim they don't want it, but are mad at everyone who has more than they. We call them "envious," but they are really the greedy in disguise.

But, are we greedy? Am I? Are you? Here's one way to measure our greed-quotient. We have two lists: one is marked "needs;" the other, "wants." The need list is relatively short. The want list is infinite. Every time we increase our riches, we move "wants" over to "needs."

Example: There was a time we wanted a car. We *needed* transportation. We *wanted* A/C, cruise-control, power steering, i.e., "the Options," but we didn't *need* them. Now they're no longer options but needs.

We're greedy when *enough* is always "a little bit more." Which means, of course, that we are *all* greedy. The only cure for our greed is mentioned in the ancient Proverb: *Honesty* ... with ourselves, in our getting and accumulating.

If we are honestly hungry, we can enjoy. If not, plenty is never enough.

Tolstoy asked the question: "How much property does a man really need?"

The answer? "Not very much. Just a small piece, six feet by three feet by six feet."

We have two lists: one is marked "needs;" the other, "wants" … Every time we increase our riches, we move "wants" over to "needs."

~Gerald Mann

Proverbs 10:5

A wise person gathers the crops
when they are ready.
A fool sleeps through the harvest.

18
Don't Sleep Through the Harvest!

Wisecrack

*Those who prosper from what they grow
know when to plow, to weed, to sow.
But keener yet is their eye for the time
when the flowers have fallen and the
seeds are prime.*

What an innocuous instruction! Sounds like the doting mom who always sends her brood off with a "Be careful!"

No one who's been near a farm, orchard or garden needs to be reminded to get ready for the harvest. The entire growing process is aimed at the time of reaping. To sleep when you should reap is an absurd thought!

Not so absurd, however, when you apply the advice to something besides farming. We regularly sleep through great moments from which we could be reaping quantum benefits—mentally, relationally and spiritually.

The difference between those who reap great benefits and those who "die on the vine" is often simply a matter of "wakefulness."

How many poets, painters or otherwise productive people have *never* been because they "slept through the harvest"? Kemmons Wilson, the founder of Holiday Inns of America, used to say, "There are two ways to get to the top of an oak tree: sit on the acorn until it grows, or climb it!"

The difference between those who reap great benefits and those who "die on the vine" is often simply a matter of "wakefulness."

~Gerald Mann

Proverbs 10:11a
Words that bless are a fountain of life.

19
Affirmation or
*In*firmation?

Wisecrack

Of all the voices that determine the choices
we make in our voyage through the vale,
the ones that affirm us
when the rest would "infirm" us
are the prow that pierces the gale.
For the grit of the saint to walk and not faint
is not had by probing and guessing.
He hears from within, and above the din,
that constant refrain of glad blessing.

The deepest principle of human nature is the
craving for praise.—William James.

Why do we know James' statement to be true and yet
ignore it?

Someone has postulated that by the time children
reach age 10, they have heard nine *in*firming comments

79

(criticisms, put-downs, lectures) for every affirmation (attaboy, appreciation, encouragement). By the time we reach adulthood, some say, one *in*firming comment can cancel 17 affirmations.

Proverbs 10 is about the tongue's power to bless or to curse. This chapter tells us almost everything we learn today from modern researchers. And verse 11 says it all: Affirming words are a fountain of life. *In*firming words are a cesspool—a breeding place— for violence.

Humans' inhumanity to humans lies dormant in the sewer of *in*firming words ... words that destroy self-worth. But more on that later.

The obverse is also true. The wellspring of all that is good in the human spirit is the voice that blesses. Sometimes, a person can overcome mountains of negative programming if he can hear one word of blessing.

Jesus came up from the river following his baptism and heard a voice from heaven saying, "Look at my beloved child, who brings me great delight."

Then he was led into the wilderness to see if the voice of blessing could be extinguished by all the seductive voices to the contrary. He passed the test, because he kept hearing that constant refrain of glad blessing.

Why do we ignore the power of words to bless? Because we haven't heard them ourselves. We can't *give* what we don't *have*.

The wellspring
of all that is good
in the human spirit
is the voice that
blesses. Sometimes,
a person can overcome
mountains of negative
programming if he
can hear one word
of blessing.

~Gerald Mann

Proverbs 10:11b
Words that curse are a cesspool of violence.

20
The Tale of Ozzie Rabbit

Wisecrack
When I was a kiddie,
I learned a wee ditty
to ward off glib demons of verse,
whose words are an arrow
that pierces the marrow
of the souls they are wanting to curse.
"Sticks and stones," the ditty intones ...
and you know the words that follow.
But if you've put them to use
against verbal abuse,
you also know they are hollow.

Whoever wrote, "but words can never hurt me" was deaf.

There are countless souls who never felt a single blow from paddle, strap or fist, yet their creativity and hope have been "fetal-positioned" by one good tongue-lashing.

"Ozzie Rabbit," they called him in sixth grade.

When he complained to his emasculating mom, she said it was an apt description. He was, after all, skinny and weak, and his ears were the only full-grown appendage he had.

That's where it all began.

It ended when he sent a bullet speeding through the beautiful and bright brain of the founder of America's Camelot. "Ozzie" was short for Oswald.

Your mouth can be a fountain, or a sewer line.

𝒯here are countless souls who never felt a single blow from paddle, strap or fist, yet their creativity and hope have been "fetal-positioned" by one good tongue-lashing.

~Gerald Mann

Proverbs 10:27
Reverence enriches your life,
no matter how long you live.
Irreverence kills you before you die.

21
To Die Before You Die

Wisecrack

I'm afraid to die, 'tis true—
no need to posture otherwise.
And daring to live is frightful, too;
that I shan't disguise.
But the thought which more doth terrify,
is that I should die before I die.

All so-called "lifestyles" eventually line up on one side or the other: living reverently or living irreverently. To live reverently means to seek to connect with the ground, the source, of reality beyond our own meager comprehension. To live irreverently is to cast your lot with the here and the now and the consumable, "to grab for all the gusto" because you "only go around once."

Fear drives the irreverent life; it races the clock and can't "go gentle into that good night" of death. And to live in fear is to be dead already. It is to die before you die.

To live reverently is to live before you live!

Proverbs 11:10-11, 14

The moral character of a nation is reflected
in the moral character of its leaders.
For example, a strong nation
venerates only those who have
risen to prominence by honest means.
Furthermore, it accepts leadership
only from those who practice
right-living in their private lives.
In other words, a moral nation knows it
will fail unless it's led by honest people
surrounded by honest counselors.

22
We *Do* Elect Ourselves

Wisecrack

"Throw out the rascals," is a common refrain
when we know the nation's askew.
When hell's breakin' loose, and
we're under the strain, we'll settle for anything new.
So we jump on the wagon of those who are braggin'
they'll restore our dreams of past glory.
But after a while, we see through the guile,
and we know it's the same old story.
When will we choose to expose the ruse
that our leaders set moral direction?
They're only the mirrors of the ones they serve.
We are their truest reflection.

As chaplain of our state legislature for more than two decades, I've seen the democratic process from the inside—seen the wheeling and dealing that keeps TV pundits employed.

All in all, it's my conviction legislatures are indeed representative bodies, *in every way!* Intellect, integrity, work ethic—you name it. The entire spectrum is there. From the slime to the sublime, we get what we vote for.

Thirty years ago, Solzhenitsyn accused us of being a nation that equates what's *right* with what's *legal.* He said we acknowledge no morality apart from what the law says. If it's legal, it's right. The only thing worse, he said, was the totalitarian system of his birth (USSR), where citizens had no laws to protect them.

Well, he's gone back to Russia now. Good riddance! America wasn't ready for him then, and it isn't now.

Do we really want leaders who have enough moral backbone to vote against our private interests? I don't. I'd prefer that the government raise *your* taxes and cut *your* pork—but leave *mine* alone!

Solomon poses some haunting questions for us all.

1. *Do we venerate (make a celebrity of) only those who've acquired power honestly?*

2. *Do we accept leadership only from those with personal integrity, no matter their ability to get the job done?*

3. *Do we really believe the future of our country depends on the personal integrity of our leaders?*

All in all, it's my conviction legislatures are indeed representative bodies.... Intellect, integrity, work ethic~ you name it.... From the slime to the sublime, we get what we vote for.

~Gerald Mann

Proverbs 12:1

If you love knowledge,
you want to be told when you are wrong.
If you love stupidity, you hate
to be corrected.

23
When the *Quo* Loses Its Status

Wisecrack

They taught me how to count and spell
and how to keep the wards of hell
from nibbling at our holy creed.
So, as the heir of truth well-proved,
I resolved to be unmoved by fear
or fact or doubt's bad seed.
But in the twilight of my long defense,
I'm sometimes haunted by the sense
that what I called my "education"
was that reinforced stupidity,
by name, "indoctrination."

Education is the alteration of prejudices. I am educated when I allow myself to be corrected.

Indoctrination is reinforcement of prejudices for the sake of maintaining power. It's goal is to stop change, to freeze truth in time ... to defend the *status quo* ...

even after the *quo* has lost its status!

A person or a society is in trouble when it comes to hate correction, when being *correct* is more important that being *corrected*.

Political and religious systems are most vulnerable to this reinforcement of stupidity. In their thirst for absolutes, they often forget the most obvious of all absolutes—*change.* Death and taxes are no more certain than change.

God and our Constitutional guarantees of freedom may never change, but our understanding of them *must.*

A person or a society is in trouble when it comes to hate correction, when being correct is more important than being corrected.

~Gerald Mann

Proverbs 12:9

Better to be a nobody with plenty
than to be a somebody with nothing.

24
The Best of All Worlds

Wisecrack

Two sirens were eager to claim us:
their names were Rich and Famous.
And we could not resist their pleas,
for we'd sworn an oath to have them both
when we launched on freedom's seas.
But when they were captured,
we were far from enraptured
and discovered, to our chagrin,
that taken together, they became a tether
that made us prisoners again.
Fame brought intrusive adoration,
and riches, incessant litigation—
which brings us to this terse summation:
If you want to remain autonomous,
seek to be rich and anonymous.

Imagine you have the following choices. Which would
you rather be: (1) rich and famous; (2) poor and anonymous; (3) poor and famous; or (4) rich and anonymous?

Which of these is worst? No. 2, of course—poor and anonymous. Man *does* live by bread alone, if he has no bread and no one knows it ... or even cares to ask him!

Which is best? Solomon says No. 4—rich and anonymous. Do we really believe this? It doesn't appear so. Despite our preachments to the contrary, No. 1—rich and famous—seems to be our prize. In fact, it's virtually impossible for us to view fame and fortune as separate values. They are Siamese twins. Our fortune tells us who we are. We *are* what we possess, our *things*.

Of course, we're ashamed of these values. That's why wealthy people continually tell us the responsibility that comes with keeping their wealth robs them of the fun of it. Others are quick to disavow the slightest interest in being wealthy.

Methinks they doth protest too much! Still others berate the wealthy incessantly, proving the adage that we tend to criticize most in others what we ourselves secretly lust for most.

Being rich and anonymous evades these unhealthy attitudes. It takes away snobbery, ostentation and conspicuous consumption—all of which create class warfare. It makes the wealthy more generous because they live with fewer toys. It also purifies their motives for giving because their gifts are kept secret.

Of course, there's always the IRS. Even rich and anonymous has its limits.

If
you want to remain autonomous, seek to be rich and anonymous.

~Gerald Mann

Proverbs 12:13, 16, 23

The foolish talk their way into trouble;
the wise talk their way out of it.
The foolish blow up at the slightest insult;
the wise save their ammunition.
The foolish use talk to show their ignorance;
the wise use silence to show
their intelligence.

25
Your Most Powerful
Body Part

Wisecrack

*The tongue is the tool that is used by the fool
to set his ignorance a-glistening.
The ear is the spear that is used by the seer
to change the world by listening.*

The best way to change an opponent's mind is with your
ears, by listening. Not merely to the words, but to the
message behind the words. People rarely mean what
they say. They mean what they mean.

For example, a fourteen-year-old girl has reached
puberty, but at a time in history when adolescence
(dependency on parents for livelihood) lasts into a
child's 20s. In another time, she would already have
been a bride. Now she is a woman trapped in a
dependent's body.

And her problem? Her parents "won't listen to her."
She wants to date ... older guys, of course. The guys

her age are shorter, pimplier, sillier. Her parents have the same complaint. They've told her "a thousand times, but she won't listen."

I listen. Both she and her parents say words to me. Endlessly, repetitively. I say nothing in reply. What's to say? It's hell being 14, and it's hell being the parent of a 14-year-old.

In spite of my silence, they say I'm helping them a lot. I'm "wise," according to them. You don't get it? Tell me about it.

I'm listening.

People rarely mean what they say. They mean what they mean.

~Gerald Mann

Proverbs 13:12

Dashed hopes drain the heart dry,
but one dream come true is a tree of life.

26
Dreams that Always Come True

Wisecrack

Falser words were never spoken,
than those which say that hearts get broken.
Hearts don't break like pot or pane,
but, starved for hope, they slowly wane.

There's nothing like a good break to restore all of our
dashed hopes and dreams. "One dream come true," is
all we need, says Solomon.

It set me to thinking. If Solomon is correct, are there
any dreams that *always* come true? There are at least
three.

1. *If your dream is to become rich by giving,*
your dream will always come true! If your dream is
to become rich by *getting,* you'll never get enough
... or if you do, you'll become poor protecting it. When
you *give,* you're declaring you have enough to let some
go. It means you're rich.

105

If you're too poor to be generous, you'll always be poor. (I know some poverty-stricken millionaires.)

2. *If your dream is to become happy by helping others, your dream will always come true!* When you help someone, you're using your power. If you have the power to help, you're not weak! Do you get it? Helping makes you focus on your strength, not your weakness. On the other hand, if your dream is to become happy by *using* others, you'll never be happy ... others cannot make you happy! You'll use them up and have to find others.

3. *If your dream is to become fearless by trusting God, your dream will always come true!* Fear is the root cause of all human evil and self-destruction. There's only one way to become fearless—trust something that will not let you down. Look around for an ultimate security in which you can place your trust.

If you find something more dependable than God, let me know!

*Look around
for an ultimate
security in which
you can place
your trust. If you
find something
more dependable
than God, let
me know!*

~Gerald Mann

Proverbs 13:24

A refusal to correct is a refusal to love.
Love your children by correcting them.

27
First Amendment Parenting

Wisecrack

"Spare the rod and spoil the child!"
Our forbears heeded this advice:
kids were paddled when they were wild
and coddled when they were nice.
Then Spock brought in the Age of Reason
and we put away the rod.
To strike a child was deemed a treason,
an affront to nature and to God.
But reasoning with toddlers took its toll,
and we spawned a generation bereft of self-control.
So now the age-old question has raised its head again.
"Is there a place for corporal punishment
in parental discipline?"

We humans have a habit of letting emotional reactions drive our so-called "rational" debates. Nowhere is this more evident than in the argument to spank or not to spank. We see a "Big Person" strike a "Little Person," and the argument is on! Each side recollects childhood beatings and long-simmering resentments—or else "spankings that taught me how the real world works!"

No need to list the arguments here. Anyone with average intelligence can press them. The real issue too often gets discarded: *What is discipline?* It's what we do to get from where we are to where we're meant to be ... from here to there.

An undeniable law woven into life is that either we grow from here to there, or we suffer the consequences of our unfulfillment. If we don't discipline ourselves from within, we'll be disciplined from without. We cannot get away with refusing to unfold. Punishment, then, results from our refusal to grow. It emanates from our own choices. It is not imposed from without. It is a consequence. Certain actions or inactions create certain consequences.

When applied to parenting, discipline is helping children get from here to there. It is refusing to let them stop or stray from becoming what they can be. If discipline is retribution, it *is* evil. If spanking is a parent's way to win, to vent anger or to be somebody, it *is* demonic. The key ingredient in parental love is empowering children to become what their potential allows.

However, there is a sick symbiotic substitute called *enabling. Empowering* parents set boundaries that, when crossed by the child, brook inevitable mid-course corrections. *Enabling* parents abandon children to the predations of others and themselves, all in the name of "children's rights."

The refusal to correct children is simply another example of a twisted notion that *freedom* means the freedom to *use* a person without being responsible for his or her development. Along with "First Amendment" love (sex without marriage) and divorce (when in doubt, bail out), we now have "First Amendment" parenting: Love 'em by letting 'em go … at age two!

To spank or not to spank—that is *not* the question. Perhaps, "To guide or not to guide?"

The key ingredient in parental love is empowering children to become what their potential allows.

~Gerald Mann

Proverbs 14:4

Where there are no oxen, the stable is clean,
but a good harvest requires
the strength of the ox.

28
Endure the Manure!

Wisecrack

All successes are attended by messes,
an unsavory factor, but sure.
So, if the harvest is ripe and an ox is your tractor,
you'd better grow fond of manure.

Endure the manure! (Don't get excited. I've already copyrighted the T-shirt and bumper sticker.) But I must give credit to Solomon. That's what this little Proverb is telling us. You can have a clean stable by getting rid of your ox, but then you'll have a lean harvest as well. If you want a bountiful harvest, endure the manure!

Apply this concept to marriage. *What does it mean to "endure the manure" in marriage?* It means resolving conflicts one at a time as they arise.

"That's hard work!" you say. Yes, things worth having usually require hard work. ETM!

Same goes for a successful career—ETM! Do easy things perfectly, and you'll develop the skills to do difficult things easily. Work till five on Fridays while everyone else is knocking off. As Wordsworth put it,

> *Heights of great men, reached and kept,*
> *were not attained by sudden flight.*
> *But they, while their companions slept,*
> *were toiling upward in the night!*

Endure the manure!

For a successful spiritual life, Endure the Manure means, when you pray, listen for thirty minutes instead of begging for three. It means, make God your 10-percent partner on payday. It means loving the unlovable.

All successes are attended by messes—ETM!

Do
easy things perfectly, and you'll develop the skills to do difficult things easily.

~Gerald Mann

Proverbs 14:8

What makes a wise person wise and a
foolish person foolish?
Simply this: A wise person sees pitfalls
and avoids them, and a fool
finds them by falling in.

29
Dodging the Potholes

Wisecrack

Fools can be smarter than the wise ever dreamt,
yet never complete anything they attempt.
Their problem is a lack of discernment,
the art of reading fate's map,
an awareness of pending internment,
before you're caught in the trap.

The Lord's Prayer instructs us to pray "Lead us not into temptation." This is confusing. How could God tempt us and then blame us for giving in?

The confusion is caused by the King James English, not by the meaning of the original text. Translated in today's vernacular, it would read, "Don't let us fall into the unseen potholes that lie ahead."

Dodging the potholes. Why do some of us do this more easily than others? Solomon says the reason has to do with wisdom. Remember the definition of *wisdom*? Intelligence subjected to reverence ... spirit-smarts, over street-smarts and book-smarts.

Spirit-smart people have an extra microchip in their radar. They anticipate the consequences of their actions several steps ahead. Just as a good chess player sees several moves ahead, the wise have the gift of seeing further down the road.

Of course, this sounds "preachy" to us moderns. We have come to believe that the best way to acquire wisdom is by making mistakes ... one learns where the potholes are by running into them. Wisdom is attained only by trial and error.

Solomon would disagree. He would call our way gaining *experience*, not gaining *wisdom*.

Any fool can learn where the potholes are by falling into them.

Any
fool can
learn where
the potholes
are by falling
into them.

~Gerald Mann

Proverbs 14:10
Every heart has its own bitterness
and its own joy that
no stranger can share.

30
Things I Tell Only to God

Wisecrack

There are joys I long to share,
and hidden hurts my soul would bare.
But in my heart I keep a room
to hide my gladness and my gloom.
For you cannot my feelings own,
even if I make them known.
Nor can I know your weal and woe.
It's through your own vale you must go.

There are joys and sorrows that cannot be shared with other people. You can describe the circumstances that make you sad or glad, but you can't transfer the feelings that go with them.

Remember this when you're grieving. There will come a time when family and friends will have given you all the support they can give. Your world has stopped, but theirs goes on. And they don't—they *can't*—feel your loss as you feel it.

You'll be alone with your grief, to process it or to

let it paralyze you. As the old spiritual says,

You have to walk that lonesome valley.
You have to walk it by yourself.
Nobody else can walk it for you ...

Likewise, it's futile to attempt transferring your joys intact and uninterpreted. About all you can offer is a weak, "Guess you just had to be there...." Joys are unique treasures we can take out of our memory vaults and recount from time to time. But they just don't have the same value to others.

Nevertheless, we should be grateful that both our griefs and our joys cannot be transmitted, for it means that each of us is like no one else. We are the private depositories of the sacred.

God alone can feel what we feel ... and He does. Share your secret joys and sorrows with Him.

There are
joys and sorrows
that cannot be shared
with other people. You
can describe the
circumstances that
made you glad or sad,
but you can't transfer
the feelings that
go with them.

~Gerald Mann

Proverbs 14:34

God-devotion makes a nation strong.
God-avoidance leaves people weak.

31
Values Without a Valuer

Wisecrack

When a nation is strong,
right and wrong
rarely require a debate.
When a nation is weak,
the people will seek
moral definitions from the state.

It would seem virtues and values have made a comeback at the close of the 20th century. Books, talk shows, movies—even "Sit-Com Alley"—are cashing in on the resurgence of "ethical concern."

But don't hold your breath for the next Great Awakening. Look instead at *who* is defining right and wrong —good and bad, vice and virtue.

We've mentioned the NeoCollege of Cardinals (the Supreme Court). Add the U.S. Congress and 50 state legislatures. In other words, add "the State."

In A.D. 313, Constantine made a deal with the Church. The state would keep law and order and protect the

Church as it defined right and wrong. The Renaissance and the Reformation democratized these authorities in defining vice and virtue, but as long as one religious ethic held a consensus, the Constantinian contract held in the West.

Now, pluralism reigns supreme, and the populace ignores the Church's definitions. Right and wrong—values—have been separated from a commonly shared Supreme Valuer. In fact, extreme efforts are made to avoid mentioning God at all ...

... all of which leaves the defining of right and wrong to—who else?—the State, which arrives at moral conclusions via opinion polls!

Don't hold your breath for the next Great Awakening. Look instead at who is defining right and wrong.... Pluralism reigns supreme, and ... values have been separated from a commonly shared Supreme Valuer.

~Gerald Mann

Proverbs 15:8

God is unable to answer fake prayers,
but He delights in people who
level with Him.

32
Prayers
God Can't Answer

Wisecrack

When I listened to the way I prayed,
it sounded not like me,
but like some British poet from 1683.
There were many Thees *and* Thous,
and even one to whit.
(Now, where'd I get the notion
that the Almighty is a Brit?)
Yet even stranger still
was how I begged and pleaded.
Did I believe that God knew not
exactly what I needed?
But most of all I was appalled
by how I played the role
of a sanctimonious pilgrim
who'd purified his soul.
Did I really think that I could run
an undetected scam
on a God who knows and loves me
just the way I am?

Prayer is leveling with God, plain and simple. It is not a persuasive technique whereby we get God to change the world to fit our desires.

No one can pray more powerfully than anyone else, if "more powerfully" means the ability to get God to do what others can't!

In fact, *that* is exactly the definition of pretentious praying. To pretend prayer is a magic art, performed best by professional practitioners, is voodooism.

Prayer is not some magic hidden weapon possessed by the righteous. It is a coming clean before God. It is requesting that He change *you* to fit your reality, to play the hand you're dealt with nerve and grace ... and to be with you in the fight.

This kind of praying makes God's own heart dance with delight. It's the only kind of praying He *can* answer.

No one
can pray more
powerfully than
anyone else, if
"more powerfully"
means the ability
to get God to
do what others
can't!

~Gerald Mann

Proverbs 16:2

All of the ways of a man
are clean in his own eyes,
but God weighs our true spirits.

33
Afraid to Weigh

Wisecrack

In every generation there's a pot a brewin'
o'er the moral decay that's leadin' to ruin.
Rumor is that we're close to returnin'
to the ways that first set hell to burnin.'
This doomsday cry is unrelentin,'
yet no one's willin' to start repentin'!

As Robert Burns sat in church as a child, his view was
blocked by the elegant neck and Sunday hat of a pious
lady. While he studied her nape, he saw a louse dart in
and out of hiding in her hair.

There his ode "To a Louse" was born, with its
immortal lines:
Oh wad some power the giftie gie us
To see oursels as ithers see us!
Indeed! And would some gift the Giver gie, to see
myself as *He* sees me!

You see, it really doesn't matter how *you* see me.
Your vision is as blurred as mine. Besides, if you told

133

me how I truly am, I would rush to defend myself against your accusations. (As my friends in AA say, "What you think of me is none of my business.")

And what *I* think of me is deceiving. While I know I'm a sinner, I don't think of myself as a very big sinner. As Solomon says, "We see all of *our* ways as clean." True, the world is going to the dogs, but *I'm* not part of the problem!

We're afraid to allow God to weigh us—morally—and that's too bad. It's only by looking at ourselves through God's eyes that we gain the moral nerve to change.

To *repent* means to "turn from" our wickedness, but it also means to "turn to" a loving Father who can do something about our weakness.

Our house is not hell. It's heaven.

It's only by looking at ourselves through God's eyes that we gain the moral nerve to change.

~Gerald Mann

Proverbs 16:3
Turn your ambitions over to the Lord,
and you will be a success.

34
Prospering God's Way

Wisecrack
*If you would seek that sacred space
where you were meant to be,
there's a surefire way to find your place
and fulfill your destiny.
Ask a simple question
of each path before it's trod:
"Must I go this way alone,
or can I take my God?"*

If you truly believed you're an accident born in a self-created universe, you'd have already put down this book. To believe in God at all is to believe you have a destiny. You were created for some reason.

Of course, from the very first moment you believed this, you've been troubled. *What am I to do? Where am I to go? Am I wasting my life?* Woulda ... coulda ... shoulda ...

Solomon was one of the most successful persons who ever lived. He extended the borders of his country to unprecedented lengths. He consolidated peace. He built the Temple and the national identity.

And the key to his success? It's in the one little proverb just stated. He "rolled his plans over upon the Lord."

You can read all the success manuals you like, but if success means fulfilling your destiny, the question is: *Can I roll my ambitions over upon God?*

If my ambitions are transferable to God, they are legitimate ambitions indeed.

Could God become a partner and investor in *your* business?

Ask a simple question of each path before it's trod: "Must I go this way alone, or can I take my God?"

~Gerald Mann

Proverbs 16:31
Gray hair is a glorious crown
if it comes from a struggle to do right.

35
Keep a "Clear" Head

Wisecrack

When I look at my reflection,
it says, "You're really getting old!
Your chest has fled to your midsection.
Your hair is silver instead of gold."
But I reject the mirror's knell of my mortality.
My belly stands for eating well,
and my hair—morality.
No! I haven't reached the goodness
for which I long have striven,
but every thread in my hoary head
represents a sin forgiven.

Hair does not turn gray. It turns clear! When I first read this, I was taken with the symbolism of it. Especially in view of what the ancient proverb says about gray hair. It is a crown of glory ... if it comes from outliving our sins and flaws. It is a sign that God "clears" our record, whenever we ask Him to.

I suppose this speaks to me because my hair turned

white prematurely. Science would say it is in my genes. I come from a long line of snowheads. But I also come from a long line of hearty sinners. I have done very little of anything *moderately* in my life.

The Bible tells us that God knows each of our sins. It also tells us that He has counted our every hair. He knows the number of both. Every time I look at my hoary head in the mirror I don't think of my mortality. I think of my *morality*. Every "clear" hair represents a cleared offense.

I am not moral in and of myself. I am forgiven. And because God has removed the stain and cleared me, I can try again ... and do better.

Don't pluck those "clear" hairs. They are great reminders.

Every time I look at my hoary head in the mirror, I don't think of my mortality. I think of my morality. Every "clear" hair represents a cleared offense.

~Gerald Mann

Proverbs 17:5

If you mock the poor, you mock
the God who created them.
If you take pleasure in another's calamity,
you will be visited by your own.

36
Why Some Have It Better? Worse?

Wisecrack

Two deadly sins beset our breed
and show the darkness of our greed.
One sits atop the privileged moor
and blames the poor for being poor.
The other sails in comfort's boat
o'er his neighbor's wounds to gloat.

There's a memorable line uttered at the end of an old Hollywood Western. The bad guy discovers he's been had by the good guy and questions the legitimacy of his birth by using the "B—" word.

The good guy replies, "You are correct. I am indeed a bastard. In my case, an accident of birth. But you, sir, are a self-made man!"

. · Except for movie scripts, there are no self-made people. To think otherwise is the height of human folly. Yet, we regularly lionize those who've "made it on their own"—all the while secretly congratulating ourselves for "what we've made of ourselves."

This is not just foolish pride. It is a calculated hubris—a form of God-playing. That is why the Bible is so harsh about mocking the poor. In America, such mockery often takes the form of blaming poverty on the victims. It is a way of justifying our good fortune— and our greed—by telling ourselves anyone could have what we have if they wanted it bad enough to work for it.

Gloating is another subtle form of greed. When I gloat (and I do), I'm celebrating the fact that I have more than someone else. Furthermore, I'm assuming I deserve everything that I have.

We are guilty of these sins. What can we do about them? Know them for what they are. And ourselves for what we are: broken vessels in need of redemption's mending.

Also, I constantly remind myself of these two things:

1. *I'm not fortunate because I'm C.U.T.E. (Charismatic, Unafraid, Talented and Enthusiastic);*

2. *I'm fortunate because I'm called.*

The only way to explain why some people are more fortunate and some are more challenged is that God wants both to use their circumstances as a calling, a vocation, to do something in the world for Him.

*The only
way to explain
why some people
are more fortunate
and some are
more challenged
is that God wants
both to use their
circumstances
as a calling ...*

~Gerald Mann

Proverbs 17:9

He who hides an offense
makes a friendship,
but he who fixates on an offense
loses a friendship.

37
Dump the Garbage

Wisecrack

*There's a basic rule for roofing up
a friendship from the snow.
If your pal is prone to goofing up,
simply let it go.
But if you find that you're the kind
who must challenge all offenders,
don't ever hope to count yourself
among those called "befrienders."*

I visited an inner-city church that had big garbage
cans stationed at every exit. People could leave there
every Sunday and dump their garbage on the way out.

Hypodermic syringes, freebase pipes, whiskey
bottles and notes bearing every hurt and resentment
imaginable were found in those cans.

That church was thriving in a crime-ridden area
abandoned by most religious folk.

A strong symbol!

Dumping your garbage is the healthiest thing you

can do for yourself. This is especially true with friends. The closer you get to someone, the more apt you are to goof up and hurt them, and vice versa.

Dump the garbage! Let it go! Don't sulk. Sulking and pouting is a sure sign that you haven't let it go.

Once in a rare while, you can't let it go. When this happens, tell your friend you've been hurt. Then dump the garbage.

Either way, if you ever bring that hurt up again, your friendship is ruined.

The same goes for marriages. A marriage can survive someone who gets hysterical, but not someone who gets historical—who keeps bringing up past hurts.

A marriage can survive someone who gets hysterical, but not someone who gets historical ~ who keeps bringing up past hurts.

~Gerald Mann

Proverbs 18:2
A fool does not delight in understanding,
but only in articulating his own opinion.

38
What Everyone Gives
that No One Needs

Wisecrack
The brave would find the truth,
whatever its dominions,
while cowards stay confined
to their preconceived opinions.

There's clout in honest doubt.

I don't know why religion is so afraid of it. True, there is a weakly counterfeit that isn't doubt at all. It's often found in academia, where people "doubt" to avoid committing to anything in particular. They say it's the "most intellectual" position to take.

But the heartfelt doubt that yearns to know and refuses to accept unexamined answers is the seedbed of wisdom. It is only through this kind of doubt that real understanding is ever achieved.

Where would we be if someone hadn't dared to doubt? Martin Luther, as a devout young monk, went to Rome to worship where the relics of Christ were supposedly held. He crawled up the stairs said to be transported from Pilate's fortress in Jerusalem, the same steps on which Christ had been scourged. He noticed that the stones were rather new. Then he stood up and viewed the entire Vatican compound and said to himself, "I wonder if it's so?"

That one doubt set off the Reformation.

A young Thomas Jefferson, barely in his twenties, wrote George III. How could England claim sovereignty over America's colonies, he wondered, when the English themselves were colonists recently arrived from Denmark and Saxony? King George didn't take orders from those dominions. Why should America take orders from him?

That seed of honest doubt, bravely pursued, set off the American Revolution.

Solomon, the wise, pegged the hallmark of foolish thinking long ago. A fool seeks to discover an *opinion,* not truth.

Opinions are like navels ... everybody has one. Truths are harder to come by.

*O*pinions
are like navels …
everybody has one.
Truths are harder
to come by.

~Gerald Mann

Proverbs 19:2-3

Enthusiasm without knowledge
leads to impatience, which
in turn gets people in trouble.
Some people ruin themselves
by their brashness and then
blame God for it.

39
Failing Even When God's In It

Wisecrack
The source of our failing
can be traced to an ailing
which we deny to claim,
but with deadening frequence
we follow that sequence
which is known as "Ready—fire—aim!"
And after emerging from failure's scourging
with our pride severely scored,
we seek an excuse for our self-abuse
by promptly blaming the Lord.

There is an age-old illusion that says, "Anything will succeed if God is in it!" Not true.

God was *in* the Exodus of the Israelites from Egypt, but it stalled for 40 years. He had to wait for all of the pioneers to die off before He could proceed with a fresh generation.

We persist in the belief that our sheer enthusiasm, coupled with God's will, always leads to success. And when we fail, we blame God.

Why? Obviously, because there's no one else but ourselves to blame!

In one of Charles Schultz's more famous *Peanuts* cartoons, Lucy asks Charlie Brown, "What can you do when you've really blown it, and everybody knows it, and you can't blame it on anyone else?"

"You could confess," says Charlie.

"Besides *that,* I mean!" Lucy retorts.

We're always looking for a "Besides that." In fact, this pattern is as old as time. Solomon saw it centuries ago. It's a formula: Enthusiasm minus knowledge equals impatience. Impatience leads to disaster, which in turn leads to God-blaming.

I have failed at many God-called endeavors. In every case, my abortive enterprise could be described by five adjectives: *sincere, unprepared, courageous, kind* and *sure.* (Take the first letter of each, make an acronym out of them, and see what you get!) When I have succeeded, my endeavors could be described by these adjectives: *sincere, prepared, unrelenting, nifty* and *knowledgeable.* (Work out this acronym as well.)

S.P.U.N.K. means more than enthusiastic.

We persist in the belief that our sheer enthusiasm, coupled with God's will, always leads to success. And when we fail, we blame God. Why? ... there's no one else but ourselves to blame!

~Gerald Mann

Proverbs 19:6
Many court the favor of the powerful,
and everyone is the friend
of the philanthropist.

40
He Read My Mail!

Wisecrack

I met "The Man" at a White House
meeting and sensed in him a certain sorrow.
His eyes said, "My power is fleeting,
and friends today are gone tomorrow."
So, I offered up myself as a would-be confidant,
a brother through thick and thin,
but he saw me as that dilettante
who's with you only when you win.
I became incensed that he'd reject
my votive overture
when I should've winced that he'd detect
my motive so impure.

There have been 11 presidents in the White House in my lifetime. I've shaken hands with five and visited briefly with three. Two would know me if they saw me. One I would call more than a casual acquaintance— and I didn't vote for him!

My first contact with him was in the form of a

handwritten note in which he thanked me for something
I had written. Later I was invited to the White House
to share breakfast with him and about a hundred other
men and women of the cloth.

Receiving line ... photo op ... sit down ... eat ...
brief comments by the man ... Q and A ... *adios*! This
was the routine for the morning.

I wanted more! So did every other minister in the
room. There's nothing like watching the clergy court
power ... and nothing like watching the powerful feign
being seduced.

I sensed a loneliness in the president, a yearning to
be understood as a man of spiritual proportions. I
resolved at once to be one of his champions, even though
I disagreed somewhat with his political philosophy.

I heard myself fawning over him and offering my
assistance in his "rescue from unfair innuendo and false
caricatures."

His response was glazed eyes and a well-rehearsed
brush-off. I was indignant, but I hid it well. The truth
is, he'd read my mail ... and maybe Proverbs 19:6,
too.

There's nothing like watching the clergy court power ... and nothing like watching the powerful feign being seduced.

~Gerald Mann

Proverbs 19:19

Let a person of great temper suffer
the consequences of his actions.
If you rescue him once, you will
have to do it again.

41
To Forgive or Enable?

Wisecrack

There are some who play the role of savior
by discarding the notion of recompense.
(They would destroy bad behavior
by interrupting its consequence.)
And when they're done, they seem irate
that deeds unpunished proliferate.

Love is a gift of forgiveness that empowers wrong-doers to change. In Victor Hugo's *Les Miserables*, Jean Val Jean, an escaped convict, steals silver candelabra from the house of a bishop who has taken him in. Val Jean flees but is apprehended and returned to the bishop's home.

When the police pull the candelabra from the thief's sack, the bishop says he gave them to Val Jean. The police leave. Val Jean's heart is changed. He is redeemed by the bishop's act of love.

No one is redeemed without such forgiving grace. But sometimes what we call "forgiveness" is actually *permissiveness*—a sick reinforcement of destructive behavior that enables the offender to repeat his offenses.

How do we tell the difference? When is forgiveness liberating, and when is it debilitating? When does suspending punishment redeem, and when does it only reinforce bad behavior?

According to Solomon's proverbs, the key is the offender's temperament. If wrongdoing comes from a pattern of explosive hotheadedness, we do the wrong-doer no favor by rescuing him. Instead, we must let him butt his head against the walls in order to learn where the walls are.

But if the offender is truly penitent—sorry for his offenses and ready to stop the war—forgiveness is the ultimate healer.

Until a hot head becomes a warm heart, forgiveness is permissiveness.

Until a hot head becomes a warm heart, forgiveness is permissiveness.

~Gerald Mann

Proverbs 20:14

"Bad! Bad!" says the buyer, but
when he goes his way, he boasts.

42
Helluva Deal!

Wisecrack

When I'm the buyer and you're the seller,
I tell how you're the worstest feller:
Why, you'd gouge your Ma if the price was right!
But when the deal is done and you've made the sale,
I'm moved to tell a different tale:
Why, I stole you blind in broad daylight!

Who says the Bible isn't funny?

This little proverb was written long before free-market capitalism ... but not before self-justifying consumerism!

Before we bought "it," it was outrageously priced. In retrospect, we made a helluva deal! (And even if we erred, we found a bigger sucker to take it off our hands.)

If I really want something, I can always find a way to justify the purchase.

I'm glad the proverb simply acknowledges this fact about my nature and doesn't condemn it.

Otherwise, I'd have a heavier load to carry.

Proverbs 20:25
Don't entrap yourself by making promises
to God that you can't keep.

43
Fantasy and Apostasy

Wisecrack

*All promises to God unkept
stem not from bared apostasy,
but from the dreams of hearts inept,
ensnared by fantasy.*

We labor under the illusion that we can keep any promise we make to God simply because *it's made to God!* We think He will help us keep what we cannot keep.

Although such faith is laudable, it is unrealistic.

In fact, all God-promising is tricky. Jesus once said we should not swear vows, period ("... don't swear by heaven, by earth, by your city, by your head ... just say yes or no, and keep your word.—Matthew 5:33ff).

God wants us to promise Him only one thing: that we will try to trust Him in every situation, in every decision, in the future, i.e., that we will try to remain faithful (trusting) in all things.

Many a broken soul faces each day with a burden of

171

guilt over unkept promises to God. Sad. Their problem is not apostasy, but fantasy. They've become ensnared in their own trap.

What can you do when you are so entrapped? Just walk out, shed your guilt and promise God one thing: to give it your best. God doesn't want perfection. He wants progress.

And His promise is to be there with us every time we walk into the light of a new day.

Promise God one thing: to give it your best. God doesn't want perfection. He wants progress. And His promise is to be there with us every time we walk into the light of a new day.

~Gerald Mann

Proverbs 21:1
The Lord controls the mind of a king
as easily as He directs the
course of a stream.

44
A Puzzling Presence

Wisecrack

"You say God's hand is in history?
Well, answer me this mystery:
Where was He when the Hitlers and Stalins
spilled innocent blood by the gallons?
And where was He when quake, wind and fire
piled up the corpses higher and higher?
And where was He when the dread disease
snuffed out a child with such mindless ease?"
I cannot answer your haunting question,
but I do have one simple suggestion.
Before choosing the darkness over the light
ask if God's with us in the midst of the fight.

It's virtually impossible to believe: God controls the mind of a king as easily as He controls the course of a stream.

When I see cancer slowly sapping the life of a child ... Worse still, when I read of a tyrant named Idi Amin ... I cannot reconcile the question: *If God is great and God is good, why ...?* You know the rest.

Why then do I still believe? Is it because I'm afraid to admit I'm alone in a mindless, self-creating universe? Is religion just a convenient opiate, as Marx claimed, a drug to dull the painful reality that we simply procreate, defecate and terminate?

Maybe so.

I could easily believe it except for another haunting question. *What is this presence I feel that keeps me going and loving in the midst of the void?*

How do I explain extraordinary goodness in the midst of extraordinary evil? Why does anything exist at all? Why not *nothing* at all?

At the end of the day, I'm faced with a mystery more puzzling than the mystery of surd evil: the mystery of that power I call God's grace.

And after experiencing that power firsthand, I wonder if this proverb means that the king, in all of his evil machinations, eventually is swallowed up by God's overall plan to reconcile the world to Himself?

Frankly, this makes as much sense as the beliefs of nihilism. Not more, but as much.

And so, we are left to choose—to aid and abet the good ... or the bad.

What is
this presence
I feel that
keeps me going
and loving
in the midst
of the void?

~Gerald Mann

Proverbs 21:14
You can defuse your enemy's anger
by giving him a gift in secret.

45
Beast to Beast?

Wisecrack

"Shoot the bad guys!" they were taught.
"A bullet's the only message understood,
and using evil against itself
is the only time that evil's good."
The good guys followed this advice
and found it quite a pleasure,
but now the list of who is who
is difficult to measure.

Even in the "eye for an eye" Old Testament, there is an awareness that the only way to eradicate evil is by responding to it in contrast.

It would be centuries before a Rabbi named Jesus would tell the world that evil used to combat evil only proliferates evil. That giving an opposite response to our enemies is the only way to defuse enmity. Yet Solomon saw the wisdom of it in this little proverb.

Don't copy your enemy's anger. Secretly send him a gift. Why secretly? So he won't immediately think you're trying to manipulate him. If you do it publicly, you only trigger his defenses. Done in secret, the gift is truly a peace offering. If your enemy has a shred of peacefulness left in his heart, he will be touched by your overture.

Returning good for evil is not senseless idealism. It is hard-nosed realism. With enemies, we have only two choices: Defeat the beast by becoming the beast, or turn it into a human being by *being* human ourselves!

Someone has to leave the last insult unanswered, the last blow unreturned. Otherwise, bestiality reigns. The people who today dwell in the land where Solomon walked could surely use a dose of his logic!

But then, so could I.

Returning good for evil is not senseless idealism. It is hard-nosed realism. With enemies, we have only two choices: Defeat the beast by becoming the beast, or turn it into a human being by being human ourselves!

~Gerald Mann

Proverbs 21:25–26

Lazy people starve themselves to death
by grieving over what they don't have,
while hard-working people regenerate
themselves by sharing what they do have.

46
Poverty and the Mind

Wisecrack

One forlorn waif peered through the glass
at the overflowing shelves
and complained of how the upper class
kept it for themselves.
Another empty pilgrim stopped and, with a stare,
said, "Nothing on this earth
can keep me outa there!"

Solomon has already warned us about blaming the poor for being poor. Indifference to the weakest among us is the hallmark of people without God and without their own humanity.

But he also repeats the theme that much poverty is caused by a particular state of mind or method of viewing reality. Some people are poor because they are preoccupied with what they don't have.

They stand at the window looking into the candy store, and all they can think of are the forces that keep them out. This attitude causes a paralysis known as laziness. In fact, it is the main cause of laziness.

Most "lazy" people aren't worthless hangers-on who want others to take care of them. Most are so focused on what they perceive to be the obstacles to prosperity that they haven't the energy to try to succeed. Their energy is drained by a constant resentment.

Others, however, look through the window and focus on how to "get in there." They usually succeed.

Case in point: America is flooded with third-world immigrants who arrive and thrive with enthusiasm, while a multigenerational underclass continues to perpetuate itself in anger and despair.

*M*ost "lazy"
people are
so focused on
what they conceive
to be the obstacles
to prosperity that
they haven't the
energy to try...

~Gerald Mann

Proverbs 22:7b
The borrower is the slave to the lender.

47
Credit Where
Credit Is Due

Wisecrack

There's a lesson, but we forget it,
that anyone who lives on credit
is choosing his master for tomorrow.
Yet since we know we'll be ruled by someone,
we go in search of that special dumb one
who'll someday forgive us what we borrow.

I disagree with those who say that Solomon forbids incurring debt here. He simply states an obvious fact: To borrow is to volunteer for servitude ... to relinquish freedom ... to mortgage your future choices.

There's nothing wrong with this, provided you're willing to abide by the realities involved. It's the denial of reality that destroys the borrower. If you don't know what you're getting into and how to get out of it, you're selling yourself into full-fledged slavery.

On the other hand, credit has its privileges. Many

mortgage holders rent money to enjoy the American dream of home, hearth and family. And most pay the rent all the way to ownership. There's no sin in lending or borrowing if we embrace reality.

But there is a sin committed blatantly in modern America: *incurring debts that others must pay,* "others" being our children.

There's nothing wrong with willingly enslaving ourselves. There's everything wrong with willingly enslaving our children.

There's no sin in lending or borrowing if we embrace reality. But there is a sin committed blatantly in modern America: incurring debts that others must pay ...

~Gerald Mann

Proverbs 22:12
The Lord Himself protects the truth,
and falsehood always exposes itself.

48
The Good News and the *Great* News!

Wisecrack

*When I was young, I tried to save
myself and God and you,
to hold the gates 'gainst evil hordes
who threatened all the true.
Now I'm old and bent and bear the many scars,
of sleepless nights and useless fights and
needless moral wars.
And so I beg to leave you with
what I wish I'd known in youth:
that evil always kills itself,
and God preserves the truth.*

The good news is, I can't save myself ... and the *great* news is, I don't have to!

I can step off the treadmill of self-perfectibility. "The beginning of wisdom is reverence for God." Solomon says that over and over in his proverbs.

Reverence, as I see it, means God's grace alone can

change and preserve me.

The good news is, I can't save you ... and the *great* news is, I don't have to! I can step off the treadmill of "Save-the-Whatever" crusades. My only task is to tell my story and leave you be.

The good news is, I can't save God ... and the *great* news is, I don't have to! I can step off the treadmill of theological correctness. What a relief! God can take care of Himself ... and the truth.

Evil's days are numbered.

And so I beg to leave you with what I wish I'd known in youth: that evil always kills itself, and God preserves the truth.

~Gerald Mann

Cross-Reference Chart

CHAPTER NO./TITLE:	SCRIPTURE:	WISECRACK BEGINS ...
1 You *Can* Begin Again!	Prov. 1:1	David saw Bathsheba bathing ...
2 Scarred Warriors Make Good Teachers	Prov. 1:8–9	When it was my turn, they tried to tell me ...
3 The Three Laws of Losers	Prov. 1:10–18	You can't peg a winner 'til the race ...
4 Get Smart or Get Wise?	Prov. 1:20–33	Those whom we dub the quick-witted ...
5 Craving What We Already Have	Prov. 2:2–9	Those who rant and pant and lurch ...
6 But the Greatest of These ...	Prov. 2:10–15	We treasure pleasure in any measure ...
7 The *Nevers* that Never Fail	Prov. 3:1–12	No matter the steepness of the climb ...
8 Being a Friend *and* a Neighbor	Prov. 3:27–32	Of all the wealth that attends our labor ...
9 It All Happens at Home	Prov. 4:1–9	"I have no bread," the father said ...
10 What Makes a Person "Good"?	Prov. 4:20–27	We awaken and ask the coming day's task ...
11 Straight Facts—Sexual Fantasies	Prov. 5:3–20	Have you paused to ponder ...
12 For Promise-Breakers	Prov. 6:1–5	Is anything worse than a promise unkept ...
13 Seven Habits of God-Feeling People	Prov. 6:16–19	For way too long, we've had God all ...
14 On Finding Decent Help	Prov. 6:6–8	How long must we suffer that incessant ...
15 No Contest	Prov. 7:6–27	In olden times we dared believe ...
16 The Real Difference Between Moms and Dads	Prov. 10:1	How different the reactions to my...

Cross-Reference Chart (*continued*)

Chapter No./Title:	Scripture:	Wisecrack begins …
17 When Plenty Is Never Enough	Prov. 10:3	Reaching for more is an unavoidable sore …
18 Don't Sleep Through the Harvest!	Prov. 10:5	Those who prosper from …
19 Affirmation or *Infirmation*?	Prov. 10:11a	Of all the voices which determine …
20 The Tale of Ozzie Rabbit	Prov. 10:11b	When I was a kiddie, I learned a …
21 To Die Before You Die	Prov. 10:27	I'm afraid to die, 'tis true …
22 We *Do* Elect Ourselves	Prov. 11:10–11, 14	"Throw out the rascals" is a common …
23 When the *Quo* Loses Its Status	Prov. 12:1	They taught me how to count and spell …
24 The Best of All Worlds	Prov. 12:9	Two sirens were eager to claim us …
25 Your Most Powerful Body Part	Prov. 12:13, 16, 23	The tongue is the tool that is used by …
26 Dreams that Always Come True	Prov. 13:12	Falser words were never spoken …
27 First Amendment Parenting	Prov. 13:24	"Spare the rod and spoil the child" …
28 Endure the Manure!	Prov. 14:4	All successes are attended by messes …
29 Dodging the Potholes	Prov. 14:8	Fools can be smarter than …
30 Things I Tell Only to God	Prov. 14:10	There are joys I long to share …
31 Values Without a Valuer	Prov. 14:34	When a nation is strong …
32 Prayers God Can't Answer	Prov. 15:8	When I listened to the way I prayed …

Cross-Reference Chart (*continued*)

CHAPTER NO./TITLE:	SCRIPTURE:	WISECRACK BEGINS …
33 Afraid to Weigh	Prov. 16:2	In every generation there's a pot a brewin' …
34 Prospering God's Way	Prov. 16:3	If you would seek that sacred space …
35 Keep a "Clear" Head	Prov. 16:31	When I look at my reflection …
36 Why Some Have It Better? Worse?	Prov. 17:5	Two deadly sins beset our breed …
37 Dump the Garbage	Prov. 17:9	There's a basic rule for roofing up …
38 What Everyone Gives that No One Needs	Prov. 18:2	The brave would find the truth …
39 Failing Even When God's In It	Prov. 19:2–3	The source of our failure can be traced …
40 He Read My Mail!	Prov. 19:6	I met "The Man" at a White House …
41 To Forgive or Enable?	Prov. 19:19	There are some who play the role …
42 Helluva Deal!	Prov. 20:14	When I'm the buyer and you're the seller …
43 Fantasy and Apostasy	Prov. 20:25	All promises to God unkept …
44 A Puzzling Presence	Prov. 21:1	You say God's hand is in …
45 Beast to Beast?	Prov. 21:14	"Shoot the bad guys!" they were taught …
46 Poverty and the Mind	Prov. 21:25–26	One forlorn waif peered through the glass …
47 Credit Where Credit Is Due	Prov. 22:7b	There's a lesson but we forget it …
48 The Good News and the *Great* News!	Prov. 22:12	When I was young, I tried to save …